I WONDER Why

Columbus Crossed The Ocean

and other questions about explorers

Rosie Greenwood

KINGFISHER

Published 2013 by Kingfisher
an imprint of Macmillan Children's Books
a division of Macmillan Publishers Limited
20 New Wharf Road, London N1 9RR
Basingstoke and Oxford
Associated companies throughout the world
www.panmacmillan.com

First published 2005 by Kingfisher

ISBN 978-0-7534-3647-9

Copyright © Macmillan Children's Books 2013

9 8 7 6 5 4 3 2 1

1TR/0912/UTD/WKT/140MA

A CIP catalogue record for this book is available from
the British Library.

Printed in China

Illustrations: Marrion Appleton 8tl; Chris Forsey 8t, 10–11;
Richard Hook 12–13, 22–23c; John James 6bl, 17tr; Peter Jones
(John Martin) 14–15m; Mike Lacey 16–17, 18–19, 22l, 23r;
Linden Artists 5br; Mortlemans/Philips 19; Alex Pang
8br; Neil Reed 24–24c, 30t; Bernard Robinson 4–5m;
John Spires 12tr; Ross Watton front cover; Mike White 9b, 19b,
23br, 25b, 26; Paul Wright 17br, 20–21c; Peter Wilkes (SGA)
all cartoons.

CONTENTS

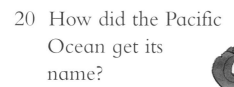

Who were the first explorers?

Over the centuries, different groups of Polynesians settled on thousands of Pacific islands.

Some of the earliest ocean voyages were made by the Polynesian peoples of New Guinea. As long as 3,500 years ago, they began leaving their homeland to explore the vast Pacific Ocean in nothing bigger than canoes.

Where was Punt?

As people sailed off in canoes from New Guinea, thousands of kilometres away in Egypt, much bigger trading ships were sent to the land of Punt. This was many kilometres south of Egypt at the tip of the Red Sea. Punt was discovered by Egyptian explorers in ancient times.

About 2,300 years ago, the Greek explorer Pytheas sailed north past Spain, France and Britain. He may have even reached Norway.

Who was Hanno?

A thousand years later, Hanno set sail from the trading city of Carthage on what is today the coast of Tunisia. Hanno was one of the first known explorers.

Hanno's ships headed west into the Atlantic then south, hugging the African coast. They may have sailed as far as the country we now call Sierra Leone.

Why did people go exploring?

Over the centuries, explorers have had all sorts of reasons for heading off on their travels. Some were looking for new lands to trade with, or to settle and farm. Others wanted to spread word of their religion. Some hoped to win fame or riches, and many simply set off in search of adventure.

Northwest Passage

CANADA

Rocky Mountains

NORTH AMERICA

ATLANTIC OCEAN

Gulf of St Lawrence

Tenochtitlan

WEST INDIES

Galapagos Islands

SOUTH AMERICA

In about the year 1000CE, a daring band of Viking explorers led by Leif Eriksson became the first Europeans to sail across the Atlantic Ocean to North America.

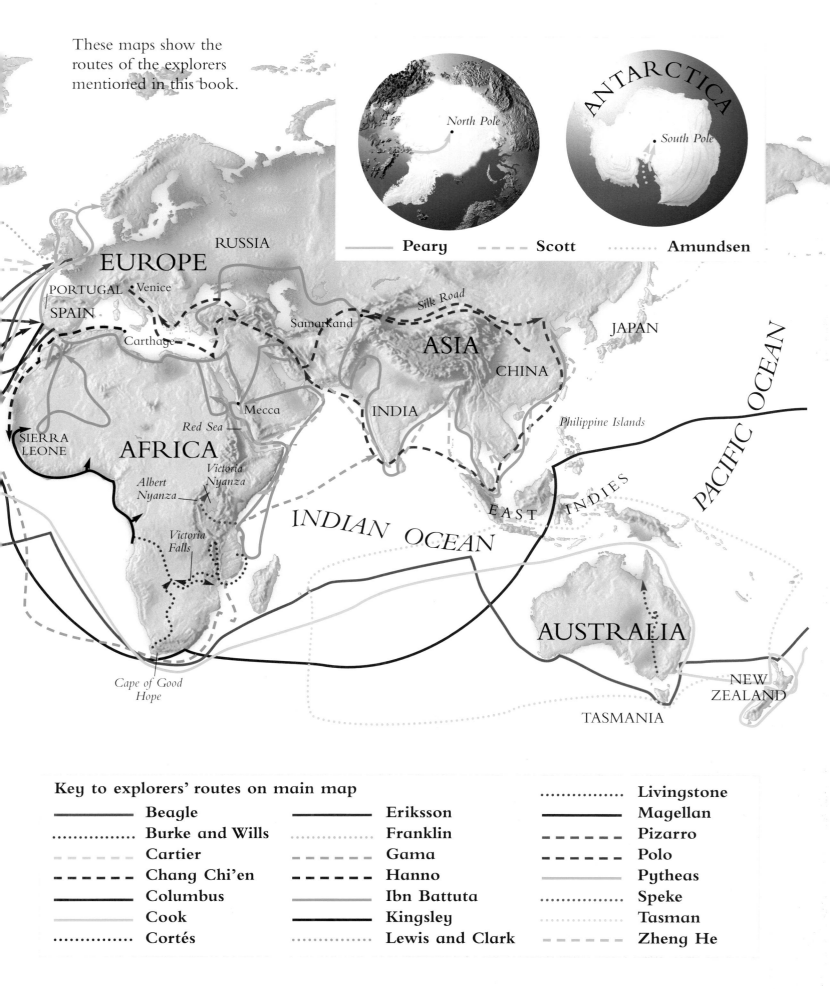

These maps show the routes of the explorers mentioned in this book.

ANTARCTICA

North Pole

South Pole

——— **Peary**   – – – **Scott**   .... **Amundsen**

RUSSIA

EUROPE

PORTUGAL   •Venice

SPAIN

Carthage

Samarkand   Silk Road

ASIA   JAPAN

CHINA

SIERRA
LEONE   Mecca

Red Sea

AFRICA   INDIA

*Albert
Nyanza*   *Victoria
Nyanza*

*Victoria
Falls*   *Philippine Islands*

INDIAN OCEAN   EAST   INDIES   PACIFIC OCEAN

AUSTRALIA

Cape of Good
Hope   NEW
ZEALAND

TASMANIA

Key to explorers' routes on main map

——— Beagle	——— Eriksson	.... Livingstone
.... Burke and Wills	.... Franklin	——— Magellan
– – – Cartier	– – – Gama	– – – Pizarro
– ∙ – Chang Chi'en	– – – Hanno	– – – Polo
——— Columbus	——— Ibn Battuta	——— Pytheas
——— Cook	——— Kingsley	.... Speke
.... Cortés	.... Lewis and Clark	.... Tasman
		– – – Zheng He

What made early explorers starstruck?

The first explorers had no compasses to help them find their way. Instead, they learned how to use the position of the stars in the night sky to guide them. The Sun's position helped them in the daytime.

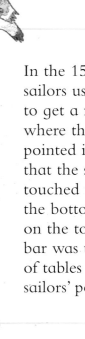

In the 15th century CE, sailors used a cross-staff to get a rough idea of where they were. They pointed it at a star so that the sliding cross piece touched the horizon on the bottom and the star on the top. A scale on the bar was used with a book of tables to work out the sailors' position.

The compass was invented in China – Chinese sailors were using it to help them find their way more than 1,000 years ago.

Early explorers worked out how fast they were travelling by timing how long it took a floating object to travel their ship's length.

Why did explorers often get lost?

Ancient maps were mainly guesswork because people knew so little of the world. World maps didn't begin to improve until the 16th century CE, when explorers made the first round-the-world voyages.

For centuries, Europeans based their maps on this one, drawn by the Greek scholar Ptolemy in the 100s CE.

When did the East discover the West?

In 127 BCE, after a long and very dangerous journey, a traveller called Chang Chi'en reached Samarkand in Central Asia. He was the first known Chinese explorer to journey outside China, and the first to learn of the great civilizations of the West, such as ancient Rome.

Soon after he began his travels, Chang Chi'en was taken prisoner by China's enemies, the Huns. It was 10 years before he escaped!

Who set sail in junks?

Chinese explorers did – junks are Chinese sailing ships. One of the greatest Chinese explorers was called Zheng He. Chinese junks dwarfed European ships by Zheng He's time, the early 15th century CE.

Zheng He's fleet of junks sailed as far as East Africa and brought home a giraffe!

Whose journey lasted 24 years?

The Arab explorer Ibn Battuta's adventures began in 1325, when he set out from his home town of Tangier in Morocco. He was so bitten by the travel bug that he didn't return home again until 1349!

Ibn Battuta wrote a book about his travels, but his memory wasn't always that good. He said he'd seen hippos with horse-like heads, and that the pyramids were cone-shaped!

What was the Silk Road?

In the centuries following Chang Chi'en's journey to Central Asia, traders began using his route to carry all sorts of luxury goods between China and Europe. Europeans named it the Silk Road, because silk was top of their list when shopping for Chinese luxuries.

Silk thread comes from the cocoons of silkworm caterpillars that munch away on mulberry leaves.

For centuries no one outside China knew how silk was made. The punishment for giving away the secret was death.

Then, in the 550s CE, the Roman emperor sent two monks to China as spies. Cleverly, they hid silkworm caterpillar eggs in their walking sticks and managed to smuggle them out of China – the secret was out!

Which Italian teenager travelled the Silk Road?

Marco Polo was only 17 in 1271, when he set out from Venice with his father and uncle. The three travellers sailed to the Middle East. Then they journeyed overland, becoming the first-known Europeans to make it to the Silk Road's end, in China.

No one knows when the Italians first made ice cream, but Marco Polo may have brought a recipe for water ices back with him from China.

Why did Columbus cross the ocean?

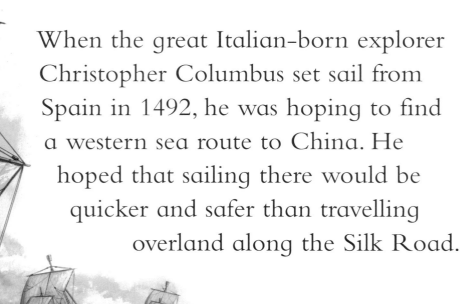

When the great Italian-born explorer Christopher Columbus set sail from Spain in 1492, he was hoping to find a western sea route to China. He hoped that sailing there would be quicker and safer than travelling overland along the Silk Road.

Like other Europeans of his day, Columbus had no idea that the Americas and the islands of the West Indies lay between him and China.

Did he find what he was looking for?

Columbus never found his western sea route. Nor did he know he had reached the Americas. He always believed that the West Indies, where he first landed, were part of Asia.

The first European to sail to India was Portugal's Vasco da Gama, in 1497–98. Unlike Columbus, he headed south around Africa and then east, not west.

What was life like on board?

Ordinary sailors ate and slept on the bare boards of the ship's deck – they had no tables and no beds. A sailor's life was hard work, with few home comforts.

Things improved after Columbus's men got to the West Indies and spotted the local people sleeping in hanging beds. The European name for this nifty invention was the hammock.

Who were the conquistadors?

In Europe, people soon realized that Columbus had stumbled across new lands they called the Americas. Rumours spread that they were rich in gold, and Spanish soldiers began heading there in search of their fortunes. The soldiers were known as conquistadors, from the Spanish for 'conqueror', because they were more interested in conquering new lands than exploring them.

Unlike Europeans, the native peoples of the Americas didn't use gold as money. Instead, they valued it for its beauty.

The conquistadors were among the first Europeans to try the tasty things that until then were only grown in South America – from pineapples, tomatoes and potatoes to chocolate.

Where was the city on a lake?

The beautiful city on a lake was Tenochtitlan, the capital of the Aztec people's vast empire in what is today called Mexico.
The conquistador Hernán Cortés was the first European to see Tenochtitlan. His army invaded and conquered the Aztecs' lands in 1519–21.

Tenochtitlan was built on islands in Lake Texcoco. Like the Italian city of Venice, it was crisscrossed by canals and streets.

In the 1530s, conquistadors led by Francisco Pizarro conquered the huge empire of the Incas, in the country that is now called Peru.

Where was New France?

In 1534, the French explorer Jacques Cartier sailed into the Gulf of St Lawrence, in what is now Canada. He claimed the land around it for his country, and the region became known as New France.

Who followed in the explorers' footsteps?

Settlers did. In November 1620, for instance, a ship called the *Mayflower* sailed into what is now Cape Cod Bay, Massachusetts, USA. On board were 102 English settlers, or immigrants, who became known as the Pilgrim Fathers.

The *Mayflower's* crew called the settlers 'puke-stockings' because they were so seasick during the crossing from England!

Who blazed a trail across the Rockies?

North America is a vast continent, and nearly 200 years passed before explorers found their way along its rushing rivers and across its mighty Rocky Mountains to stand on the eastern shore of the Pacific Ocean. The trailblazers were Meriwether Lewis and William Clark, in November 1805.

Lewis and Clark were helped by a Shoshone native American woman called Sacagawea, who acted as their interpreter.

How did the Pacific Ocean get its name?

PACIFIC OCEAN

The first explorer to find a route around the Americas was Ferdinand Magellan of Portugal. In 1519, he set sail from Spain and headed south into the Atlantic. He rounded the tip of South America just over a year later. As the ocean on the continent's far side was much calmer than the Atlantic, Magellan named it the Pacific Ocean, meaning 'peaceful'.

Magellan set out from Spain with five ships and about 240 men. Only three ships made it to the Pacific Ocean.

Sailing across the Pacific Ocean took far longer than expected. Magellan's men ran out of food and ate rats, leather and even sawdust!

Who first sailed around the world?

Magellan's expedition was the first to complete this amazing feat, but only one ship and 18 men made it safely home to Spain in 1522. Sadly, Magellan himself wasn't on board with them – he was killed by local people in the Philippine Islands in 1521.

What is the Northwest Passage?

It's a sea route around the top of North America, which was discovered in the 1840s by British explorer John Franklin. Tragically, he and his crew didn't make it all the way through the Passage – they died after their ships became stuck in the ice.

Why is Doctor Livingstone famous?

In the 1850s, the Scottish explorer Doctor David Livingstone became the first European to cross Africa from west to east. His amazing three-year journey helped make him a legend back home in Britain.

Livingstone was the first European to peer over the spectacular Victoria Falls on the Zambezi River.

Who cracked the puzzle of the longest river?

Until the 1860s, Europeans had no idea where the Nile, the world's longest river, began. Then British explorer John Hanning Speke proved that it flowed out of the vast African lake today known as Victoria Nyanza.

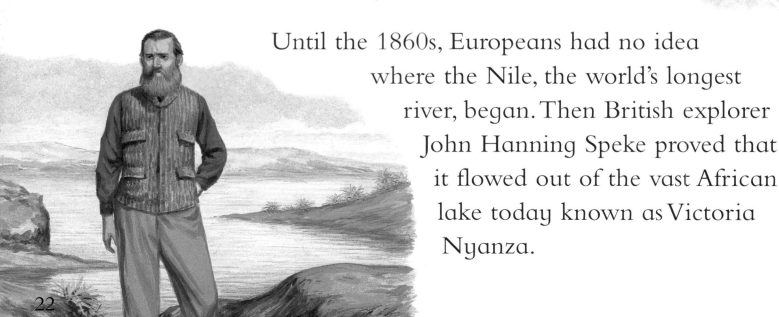

In 1864, Florence White Baker and her husband Samuel became the first Europeans to see the huge lake now called Albert Nyanza.

Why did some explorers wear dresses?

Women explorers always wore dresses! Although most 19th century explorers were men, a few brave women also set out to carve a path into the unknown. They included British explorer Mary Kingsley. In the 1890s, she put the comforts of home behind her and travelled all the way to Africa to study its people and its wildlife.

Mary Kingsley was the first European woman to climb Mount Cameroon, one of Africa's highest mountains.

Who named the kangaroo?

In 1770, British explorer Captain James Cook became the first European to land on Australia's east coast. No one is certain what the Aboriginal people called their country's unusual hopping animals – but Cook and his men believed the Aboriginal word was 'kangaroo'.

When did Europeans discover surfing?

Captain Cook and his men were the first Europeans to see anyone surfing, in 1769. The surfers were natives of the Pacific island of Tahiti.

In 1642, Dutchman Abel Tasman became the first European to visit the island off Australia's southeast tip. Today it is still called Tasmania.

On their long voyage not one of Cook's men suffered from scurvy – a killer disease caused by lack of vitamin C. This was due to their special diet, which included orange and lemon juice and pickled cabbage!

Which explorers crossed Australia?

In February 1861, Robert Burke and William Wills became the first European-born explorers to cross Australia from south to north. It took them nearly six months to complete their mammoth 3,000-kilometre trek right across the heart of the continent.

Burke and Wills had two companions, Charles Gray and John King. Only King made it home again – the other three all died of hunger in the outback.

When did the *Beagle* set sail?

A ship called the *Beagle* carried a British scientific expedition around the world in the 1830s. Exploration then was as much about discovering new plants and animals as about finding new places.

One of the *Beagle* scientists' most amazing finds was the 1.2-metre-long giant tortoise of the Galapágos Islands.

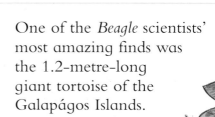

The *Beagle's* most famous crew member was scientist Charles Darwin.

Why were some explorers artists too?

Before the camera was invented, the only way to record things was to draw or paint them. Artists were key team members on the early voyages of scientific exploration.

Which explorers dived deepest?

In January 1960, Jacques Piccard of Switzerland and Don Walsh of the United States became the first-ever people to dive to the world's deepest place – the bottom of the Marianas Trench, 11 kilometres below the surface of the Pacific Ocean.

Are there chimneys under the sea?

Since the 1960s, scientists have made all sorts of astonishing underwater discoveries – including chimney-like structures that gush smoke-coloured water up from beneath the seabed!

Which explorers were first at the North Pole?

Two Americans claimed this record – Frederick Cook in 1908 and Robert Peary in 1909. No one is sure whether either man actually made it to the Pole, but most people think that Peary's claim is strongest.

Peary didn't go it alone – he took along his friend Matthew Henson and a four-man team of Inuit.

Who won the race to the South Pole?

In 1911, two teams led by Norwegian explorer Roald Amundsen and Briton Robert Scott battled to be first at the South Pole. The winners were Amundsen's men, on 14 December 1911. Their 1,300-kilometre trek across the polar ice had taken 56 days.

Scott's team finally made it to the South Pole on 17 January 1912. Sadly, all five men died from cold and hunger on the return journey.

What is a polar explorer's best friend?

A sturdy husky dog is brilliant at battling with the bitter weather of polar regions. Huskies helped give Amundsen's team the winning edge. The Norwegians used 52 dogs to pull the sledges carrying their tents, food and other supplies.

The British team tried to use ponies to pull their sledges. Unfortunately they weren't up to the job, and Scott's men ended up hauling their own sledges.

Who were the first people in space?

Russian Yuri Gagarin was the first person ever to travel into space, in April 1961. The first woman to get lift off was Russian Valentina Tereshkova, in June 1963.

Yuri Gagarin

Valentina Tereshkova

The first animal in space was a dog called Laika, in 1957.

When were the Moon landings?

The first people ever to walk on another world were Americans Neil Armstrong and Buzz Aldrin. Their landing craft touched down on the Moon's surface in July 1969.

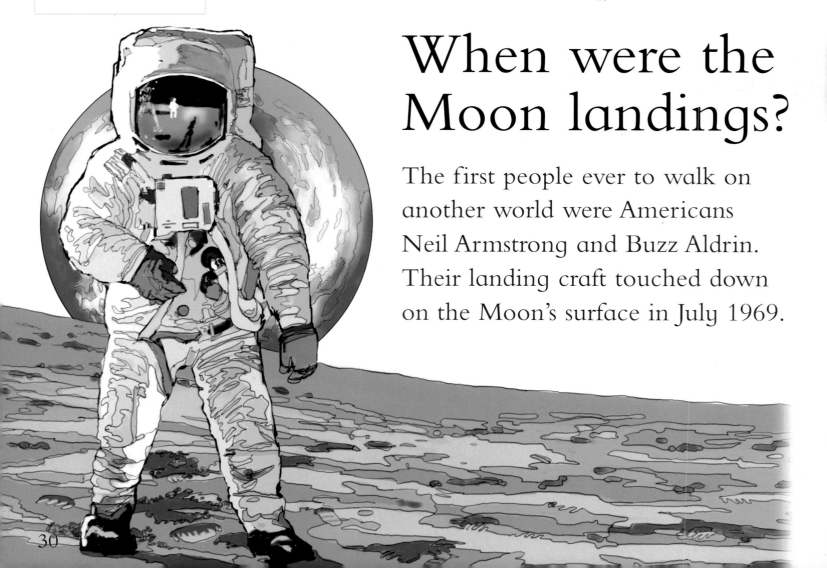

Is there anywhere left to explore?

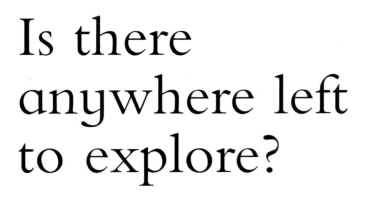

We still have a lot to learn about our planet. There are many hidden mysteries in the oceans' depths and at the frozen poles. But the biggest unsolved mysteries lie beyond Earth – space is the final frontier for modern-day explorers!

It's expensive and dangerous to send people into space, so robots are used instead. Since 1997, for instance, robot rovers have landed on Mars and explored its surface.

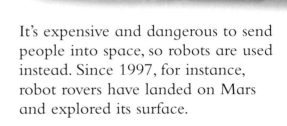

The Cassini-Huygens mission reached the beautiful planet Saturn in July 2004. Robot probes studying its rings of ice and its moons may unlock many of the mysteries of our own planet's history.

Index